UNEXPECTED JOURNEYS

Michele Hermansen

MW01657107

Unexpected Journeys

This book may not be reproduced, in whole or in part, in any form (beyond that copying permitted by Sections 107 and 108 of the U.S. Copyright Law and except by reviewers for the public press), without written permission from the author.

The author acknowledges the trademarked status and trademark owners of the brands mentioned in this work.

Copyright © **2010 Michele Hermansen**

All Rights Reserved

1st Edition Print 2010
Library of Congress Control Number: 2010922770

ISBN: 978-0-615-35476-7

Written by: Michele Hermansen
Photography by: Michele Hermansen
Author Photo by: D.H. Palmer
Back Cover Photo by: H.J. Mtisi
Cover Design & Layout: Anthony Sclavi; BRIO LLC, Minneapolis, MN

Publisher: Unexpected Journeys, LLC.
www.mhermansen.com

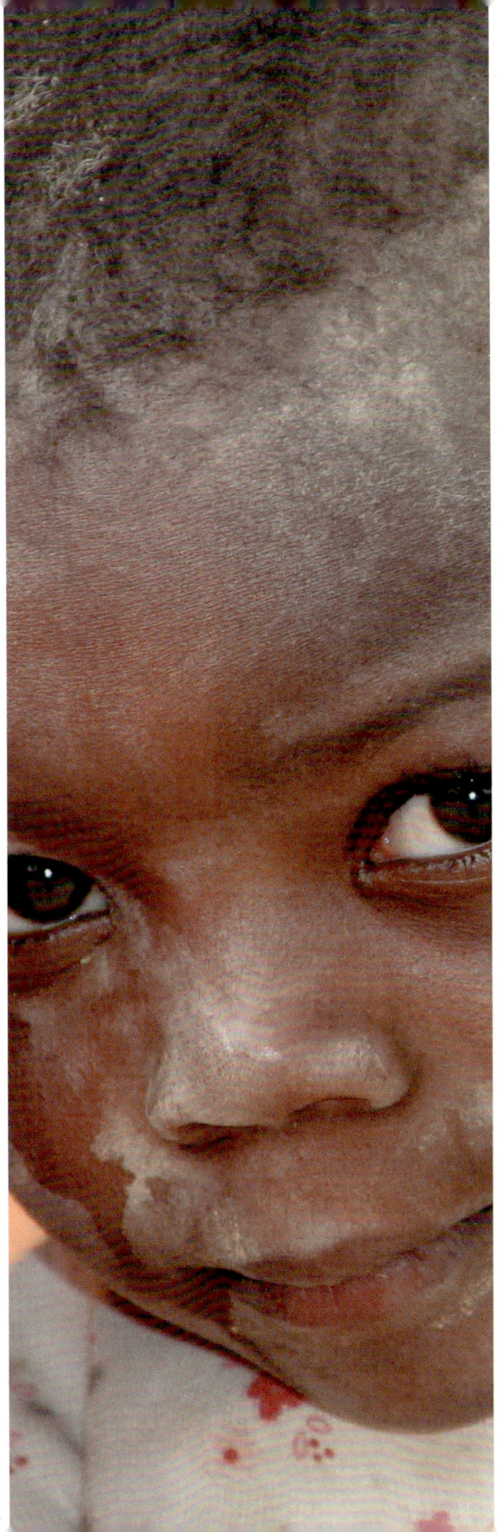

This book is dedicated to my family, related and not, for their support and encouragement:

My parents, Curt and Elaine Anderson, have given me the strong roots of faith in God and the security of a loving family. They are unequaled role models.

My husband, Jim, stands solidly with me through all the turns in the road. He dreamed for me when I had none and is there with a fresh horse when I need it. Jim, Kristi and Jacci are the stars in my sky. They embrace the unexpected journeys and share my passion.

Mick, Marin, Nancy, Kathleen, Kris, Arba-Della and Bill counsel, challenge, celebrate, console, and share the warmth of the campfire.

Control

1

Life
is not lived
in a straight line.
Even though we may know
where we think we want to go, we
may not get there—or at least not in the way or timeline that we think we will. Sometimes, it's the unexpected journeys that provide the clearest view.

When I left home that Tuesday morning, I thought I was headed for St. Louis. What I didn't realize was that I was really on my way to Africa. But in order to understand that abrupt change in direction, I need to take you back some years.

I spent the most formative decade of my career in a corporate environment that was not what we would proudly promote today

American
AA

as "family-friendly". It was the decade of the 1980's and I was one of few female mid-managers in the company. Both of our daughters were born during that time and I noted only one other woman in a visible position who became pregnant and continued in a prominent position.

It was a hard-driving, male-dominated international company. There was even a booklet that defined appropriate management behavior, from the color of the socks, shirts, suits and ties that men must wear, to the permissible things that could be on a desk top. Suit jackets were required to be worn outside of an individual office, so the sound of a coat hanger banging on the door was heard when someone was leaving their office. The handbook allowed one "tasteful family picture" on the desk. I somewhat jokingly said that since I never knew if it was supposed to be a tasteful photo or a photo of a tasteful family, I erred on the safe side and didn't put any photo on my desk. The truth, though, is that I worked very hard to ensure that neither being a female nor being a mother were ever perceived as coming in front of my professionalism. That was terrifically hard to balance when I also felt that becoming a parent should be a very deliberate decision that was taken seriously every day.

Both of our children were born on Fridays. Both times, I worked a normal day on Thursday, went into labor before dawn Friday morning, and the baby was born that day. During my maternity leaves, I took calls and routinely received my mail from work. There were no boundaries when it came to work.

I remember receiving a phone call at home at 6 a.m. one morning from an employee in Singapore. The call remains so clear because we were living in a trailer while building a house, had only one wall phone, I had just dropped a contact lens down the sink and was trying to remove the pipes under the sink with a wrench, and our oldest daughter, then 3 years old, was asking for her pancakes before going to the daycare. That picture of my humanness and the challenges of my dual roles was carefully hidden.

The skills I learned and habits I developed that allowed me to survive in that harsh environment and even thrive professionally, continued to filter the lens through which I looked and made decisions long after I left that job. I can now see a number of examples of that filter's effect on the lens through which I viewed my work life. For example, when I was nearly abducted in 1981 by someone posing as a cab driver at the Newark airport outside of New York City, I never told anyone–especially not my husband or friends–and just picked up more defensive travel habits. I successfully avoided New York for many years, and always rented cars wherever I could to make sure that I was in control, instead of taking cabs.

I was in control–strict, almost obsessive control, of my life and emotions. That was a survival tool and I realize that one way I maintained my focus and control was by burying my emotions and core under layers of armor. Impervious –that's how it looked from the outside. I learned to maintain neutral facial expression and body language, even in the most difficult situations.

UNITED
Welcome.
Thank you
for choosing
to fly with us.

Focus

2

As you may see, it wasn't unusual on that Tuesday morning that I was totally focused on getting to my scheduled meeting in St. Louis, prepared and on time. I had just been promoted to Vice President of National Sales. That week it was St. Louis, the next week Baltimore, Washington D.C. and New York City, then the following week Chicago and North Carolina. That day in St. Louis was the monthly company review for my business unit, in preparation for the monthly report to our investors, a prominent Wall Street venture capital firm.

I took an early flight out of Minneapolis, about 6 a.m., with a tight connection to a United Airlines flight in O'Hare. The United flight was in a different terminal than the arrival of my first flight, so as soon as we deplaned I ran through the airport with my roll-aboard suitcase, laptop and brief case. I arrived at my United flight as the plane was boarding and got in line. I overheard two people talking, something about a plane crashing into the World Trade Center. Looking around for a TV monitor, it was then that I realized that none of the monitors were on. "Hmmm—no monitors—that's a little curious," I thought. "That's too bad; must've been some kind of terrorism on an international flight."

We were boarding so I moved down the jetway and onto the plane. I was standing in the aisle of the plane, opposite the galley, when the flight attendant put her arm in front of me to signal me to stay there, while she picked up the microphone.

"Ladies and gentlemen, we have just been informed that all flights out of O'Hare are being held on the ground for the next 45 minutes. You are welcome to deplane if you'd like, but be sure to bring your boarding pass and remain in the gate area for further announcements."

Damn! Hold up flights out of O'Hare for 45 minutes and we'll be backed up all day. No way will I make it to St. Louis in time for our 11:00 meeting!

The man in front of me was on his cell phone, apparently to his wife. I heard him say, "OK then, I'm going to drive to St. Louis. I'll call you when I get on the road."

Impulsively I said to him, "You're driving to St. Louis? Do you mind if I hitch a ride? We'll be here all day in this mess."

He said, "Sure, we'd better get moving. It's going to get crazy in here. Oh, by the way, my name's Dave."

"Thanks, I'm Michele."

With no more information than that, we began hustling through the airport. I tried my cell phone to call the office, but the network was busy. When we passed the rental car counters, and didn't stop, I had a mini-flashback to that day in the Newark airport. I had a little twinge of "Are you crazy??? You have no clue who this guy is. What are you doing?" So I asked, "You're not renting a car?" and he said, "No, I live here. I'm parked in the lot."

I started making disciplined mental notes. I got the license plate as we walked up to the car, and wrote it down in my notebook as soon as I sat down in the passenger seat, along with the color and make of the car.

He turned on the radio as we pulled out of the parking ramp. It quickly became apparent that Tuesday, September 11, 2001 was no ordinary day in any way.

Our paths and the options we envisioned, so strong and uplifting, were irreparably scarred in an instant

Sharp Curves Ahead

3

When we were each able to get cell signals, he was on the phone to his wife, and since my husband isn't reachable during the day, I called my dad at work. I nonchalantly told him that the flights were grounded at O'Hare and I was driving to St. Louis instead. Checking to be sure that Dave was involved in his conversation, I quietly told my dad to write down the license number of the gold Toyota.

We kept listening to the radio as we drove. The events unfolding in New York were stunning. My sister called my cell phone to find out where I was. I told her I had been at O'Hare and was now driving to St. Louis and assured her that everything was just fine. She burst into tears and demanded, "We want you home!"

I assured her again that everything was fine and I needed to go to St. Louis. She said she'd call the high school to let one daughter know that I was okay, and she'd call our older daughter at college to tell her. It honestly hadn't occurred to me that anyone would be worried about me.

The towers fell in New York, and the Chicago radio station reported that the Sears Tower in downtown Chicago was being evacuated. Somewhere south of Chicago, between the cornfields that bordered the freeway, I turned to the former stranger with whom I was riding and asked, "Is there a town of any size coming up?"

He said, "No, not really. Do you need to use a restroom?"

"No…I need to go home to my family. I need to find a rental car."

He answered, "You know, I've been thinking I need to go home, too." We drove through the grassy median dividing the freeway and headed back to Chicago. I immediately started calling rental car companies, which in itself was difficult because the cell networks were jammed. All the cars were already gone. He called his wife to get the phone number of the little Enterprise lot near his home in Mt. Prospect. Even their cars were gone. He offered to take me to his home, which I declined. I told him he should just drop me off at the first major hotel we could find that was also as far away from O'Hare as possible, because that was now considered a target.

He dropped me off at a Sheraton and I got a room, but was determined not to stay. A Chevrolet dealership about 75 miles west of Chicago was willing to let me literally borrow a car, thanks to a contact from my brother. There was one cab in front of the Sheraton and the driver had a dark complexion and a strong foreign accent. With a map on the hood of the car, we negotiated a rate for him to drive me to the dealership 75 miles away. I didn't want to take his cab, but it was the best option I had. When he took my bag to put it in the trunk, I told him that I wanted to keep it with me in the back seat. I had already decided that if anything looked questionable, I would jump out of the car no matter what speed we were going. Even by then, early afternoon, there had already been references to Middle East terrorists.

In an effort to find out what my risk was, as soon as the cab pulled away from the hotel I casually asked, "So, where is your home?" I was relieved as he proudly pulled out a whole line of photos of his Russian family waiting for him in Moscow to raise the money to bring them to the U.S. Happy he was a Russian—what a contrast with the Cold War fears of my youth.

Once I got into the relative safety of my borrowed car with the assurance that I was going home, it was a long, strange and lonely drive. There were very few cars on the road, and mostly semi's. I saw one very small car with 5 people packed into it, all dressed in business suits. They had also apparently been stranded somewhere and were happy just to get any car to drive home. Around suppertime, I stopped at a Dairy Queen in southern Wisconsin. It was there, on a little TV set on top of one of their trash containers, that I first saw the TV footage of the towers falling.

While I had no way of knowing what was ahead, the road of my life started to turn that day.

Bomalang'ombe, Tanzania

Questions

4

I made it until that Sunday before the emotions burst out of my controlled, professional armor. We had gone to church as usual, and at the end of the service as people started to file out, the organist started very softly playing "God Bless America". Pretty much everyone stopped and just stood there; then people began to sing. In seconds, the tears were streaming down my cheeks and I was sobbing.

'Stand beside her and guide her through the night with the light from above.

From the mountains, to the prairies, to the oceans white with foam…'

I sobbed while I earnestly and silently prayed the words to the song.

It wasn't a song of admiration, awe or nationalism; it was a gut-level pleading with God for guidance in the darkness. I had gone through it many times before in that week, but now it was out in the open, raw and exposed.

My husband looked at me and cautiously put a rigid arm across my shoulders and walked outside without saying a word to me as I sobbed. After all, he was accustomed to my businesslike demeanor and never had to worry about public displays of affection or emotion that can be unnerving for the stoic introvert that he is. When we got outside, he tenuously asked, "Are you afraid we're going to die?"

I shook my head no, and admitted, "I don't think we're going to die. I'm afraid we're going to live, and what kind of a life is it going to be now?"

Life isn't lived in a straight line. A lot of things changed on September 11, 2001, and so did I. For the first time, it struck me that there are things I simply can't control.

I love life and I have a lot of living to do. I had planned to work hard and be responsible for my family and live a long, healthy and vibrant life. There would be time in retirement for family and friends, for travel with my husband and for adventure. There would be plenty of time to get involved in outside organizations and give back to the world as a whole. That was my plan, but some terrorists suddenly showed us that the wrong people were in control, at least for a critical few hours on that fateful Tuesday morning.

For the first time, I allowed myself to think about the "what if"... What if I don't have as much time as I expect? What if I don't get the chance to cram in all the things I want to accomplish in life, to get it all done?

Between work and immediate family, my plate had been full and even sleep sometimes seemed like a luxury. Weekends were active and devoted to doing things with my husband and daughters. There wasn't much time for others, even with a close extended family. I was generous with financial support of many programs, but personal participation was beyond my grasp until the far-off "later".

Life went on for most of us. I went back to work but something inside me was different. It was that gnawing realization that I might not have all the time in the world for the people and things that were most important. I had structured my life around responsibility and self-assurance, and all of a sudden I couldn't be confident that my input could control or even affect the outcome. I was starting to *feel*, to think more about who I was on the inside that I wanted to be on the outside.

Then in February 2004, my job was eliminated while our company positioned itself for sale. The news was delivered by phone and my severance letter was faxed because my boss was in Connecticut, the main offices were in St. Louis and I was alone in Wisconsin. The road took a sharp turn and I couldn't see anything around the corner. Without the business card and daily structure that defined me, the armor felt dented, tarnished and not so impervious.

I stayed on the road, but I wasn't singing with the radio. I got a job that could get me by, but my heart wasn't in it. Something was missing. I started trying to figure out what my purpose was and asking myself the big questions. What have I accomplished in life that really matters? Certainly we were blessed with a great family. But all that work stuff… it was so important to me and I put so much of myself into it, but in the end, what had I accomplished? What did it matter in the big picture? Sure, I got confirmation every now and then that something I did or said made someone else's life easier, but really… 5 or 10 years from now, would it matter?

The people in my inner circle –my husband, daughters, family and a few close friends –could see my struggle and didn't understand it. They kept trying to reassure me but no one had the map I needed.

The Pronouncement

5

In April 2005, a year after I lost my job, the pastor at our church announced that a team was forming to go to Africa, to a rural village in Tanzania to put in a water system. This village had no safe water or electricity and children were dying of water-borne disease. A water engineer from Stillwater and a non-profit group called St. Paul Partners thought it was an area where they could drill some wells and put in a water system. They were looking for volunteers—maybe 7 to 10 people—who could go to Africa and do this work.

The words were barely out of his mouth and I knew I was going. I was determined to be on that team. This was what I had been looking for.

There was an absolute certainty within me that I was going to Africa. This was not a life dream; it wasn't on a list of "things to do before I die". It came out of the blue but it was supremely clear. I didn't know or have the need to know the specifics. I didn't have any idea what my role would be, but I wanted to be in the thick of the work.

As certain as I was that I was going to Africa, it took me a couple of days to break the news to my husband. That's how I work on things--inside. It can be hard for people around me, especially those closest to me, because by the time I'm ready to share something I've already got it worked out. Not a great model for communication and relationships.

We had a 4-hour drive to a concert in which our daughter was performing at college, and I chose that confined environment of the car to make the announcement. I just came out with it. "You know that stuff Pastor Dan announced on Sunday about the team that's forming to build a water system in Africa? I've decided I'm going to Africa."

No response. He just kept driving. I wondered if he heard what I said and I turned to look at him. Then he said, "You don't expect me to go with you, do you?" He had lived with me long enough that he already knew the only thing that may be worth discussing was whether or not I thought he was going along. I assured him that I hadn't planned on dragging him into it, too, and that I had no problem going alone.

There may have been more to his question than either of us realized at the time, however. My pronouncement would lead to profound changes in more than just my life.

I worked through the application in my head for days. The night before it was due, I stayed up writing until 2 a.m. until I was satisfied that it was the absolute best I could do. I needed to be on the team.

Now I worried that I wouldn't make the cut. I knew I needed to go, but would anyone else know that? What did I know about water systems or third world missions for that matter? I didn't know any of the people involved and they didn't know me.

Control—it's amazing what happens when we let go and just have faith. What else could have made them leave that message on my answering machine? It said, "We're happy to tell you that you've been selected to join the Tanzania water project team. And we have a special request, but we don't want you to feel obligated. We wondered if you'd be willing to go in with the first team and home with the second team so you can document the work and the trip. It would be 22 days instead of 14, so we know that can be a lot to ask and you don't have to decide right away."

Are you kidding me? If I'm going to Africa–9,000 miles from home–just once in my life, I might as well make the most of it.

Dawn at Schiphol Airport, Amsterdam

Off the Map

6

In October 2005 I departed for Africa for 22 days, on the most unexpected of journeys.

Away from everyone and everything familiar, embarking on a physical, social and spiritual challenge with seven people whose names I barely knew. It was the beginning of a powerful change for which all of my combined life experience had been preparing me. Peeling off the armor, the invincibility, the internal demand for perfection, the acceptable structures and definitions that defined me to others, I was about to uncover the me that I was meant to be.

And that "just once in my life" phrase…it can be as much of a fallacy as "control".

I personally prepared as well as I could for the trip—attended all the team meetings, read books, talked to previous travelers to Tanzania, and searched the internet at length. Our team was "flying blind" in many ways because we had no known precedent for the type of water project we were undertaking and there were many unknowns, including some fairly basic information about the village. The two team leaders made a reconnaissance trip in June as neither one of them had even been to Tanzania before, not to mention having any first-hand knowledge of the village. As we look at it now, we realize that the success and outcome of the mission was nothing short of miraculous, with Divine intervention evident at many points.

So there I was in October 2005 in Tanzania, East Africa, bumping along in a mini-bus with 7 other people I had only met at a few meetings, going to the village of Mwatasi which couldn't be found on any map or anywhere on the internet. From the moment we drove out of Dar es Salaam after the 24 hour flight, I was just ecstatic. It was like driving through a National Geographic magazine!

But a day and a half later when we drove into Mwatasi just before dusk, it hit me. Wait a minute! Not OUR village. Yes, I had gotten all the immunizations—yellow fever, typhoid, made sure my Hepatitis A & B immunities were up to date, got my polio and tetanus boosters, and was taking my daily anti-malaria pill. That National Geographic magazine was amazing to drive through, but I wasn't going to LIVE in it for 15 days. I knew intellectually that the kids had been dying, but man, look at them! They're filthy, hacking and coughing, snot smeared on their faces. I didn't mention that I'm germ phobic, did I? Even our cat has learned that he has to be vacuumed when he comes in the house.

As I've said before, life isn't lived in a straight line. Who knows where that road will go if we're willing to take it? If I had known about some of the details, I would never have applied for the mission. Ten years earlier, I quoted the following in a note to my work colleagues as I set out on a new career path: "You cannot discover new oceans unless you have the courage to lose sight of the shore." What wonderful vistas I would have missed if I had let fear or preconceptions stand in the way of taking this journey!

I wasn't prepared for a lot of the things we found; probably none of us was. The worst thing was the rats. They were everywhere, including on our beds when we weren't there during the day. At night, we'd brush the rat poop off our beds before we rolled out our sleeping bags. I was sharing a small bed with one of my female teammates, sleeping head to toe so we'd fit.

Then one day I went back to our room to get something out of my duffel bag and a rat jumped out of the bag. I admit that I let out what might be called a blood-curdling scream that brought some nearby Tanzanians running. They were sure it was a poisonous snake, because that would be the only thing that would shake someone up so badly. Boys with long sticks were summoned to kill the snake.

There was some pretty poorly-contained laughter when they came out holding the dead rat by the neck. After all, it was just a rat, and (we were told) they're sort of like mosquitos—a nuisance that you have to tolerate because you can't do anything about them.

I had brought earplugs for sleeping, thinking that it may be tough to sleep with a bunch of strangers in fairly close quarters, especially if some of them snored. Rats running across a tin roof and wrestling in the ceiling make a whole lot more noise than people snoring. Instead of using one pair of the disposable earplugs per day, I had enough to outfit our whole team, because almost everyone was exhausted from a few sleepless nights of the rampaging rats.

Revelations

7

We were there to put in a water system because they didn't have access to safe water. But it's hard to comprehend what a hardship not having safe water is, until you see it and live it. The village of Mwatasi is in the "high country," very steep hills at about 6000 feet elevation. The village is at least 2 miles long, perched mostly along the ridge of the hills. The water sources are in the valleys below the village, from springs or little areas where water had pooled in the rainy season. It is the job of the women and children to get and carry the water for their needs each day. They walk down narrow little dirt paths to the bottom of the steep hills.

They take the bucket and swish it across the top of the water to get the big chunks of junk out of the way before they scoop the gray, dirty water to carry home.

Water is typically hauled in 4 or 5 gallon buckets, perfectly balanced on the head of a woman or child. Men do not haul water. One gallon of water weighs 8.3 pounds. A typical load of 4½ gallons weighs 37⅓ pounds.

Now imagine making a little circle out of grass or cloth to cushion your head, then lifting the full pail straight up and balancing it on the top of your head. Then, rain or shine, climb back up the steep dirt path in your bare feet to your house, start a fire and begin to make breakfast. Or if you're a child, carry the bucket on your head up the north hill to the school. Be sure you remembered your cup so you can have your ration of porridge made out of corn flour and water for lunch.

I thought I was in pretty good shape—until my first day in the village. Anywhere one goes, it's by foot. The wells were being drilled at the bottom of the hill, and we were building a pump house for the generators and equipment at the top of the hill in the center of this portion of the village. So, it was up and down the hill numerous times while we were also adjusting to the altitude. Women and children were gathering their water at the bottom of the hill and carrying it up to their homes. They walked slowly but steadily and didn't look strained.

Three of us had gone down to fill our solar showers, plastic bags that each held up to five gallons of water. I slung two filled bags over my shoulders and began the trek. As soon as I reached the first rise, I was shocked to find that I couldn't lift my leg to climb. One bag was set down so I could climb the hill with the remaining bag over my shoulder. I stopped and rested a couple times on the way up and dreaded the trip down to fetch the remaining bag. Showers moved way down the list in importance once we experienced just the fringes of life without water.

Then we started mixing concrete for the floor of the pump house. Our team demonstrated the process and then engaged the village boys and men to mix with us. Each batch was mixed on the ground with 2½ bags of cement, 10 pails of sand and 6½ pails of gravel filled with water. The gravel was bigger than desirable, but considering that it had been made by hand with very worn mauls, out of local granite-type rocks, we were fortunate to have it at all.

Even young boys could carry the heavy bags of cement on their backs. I had a tough time lifting the pails of gravel and water, and felt pain in the leg where I had broken a bone early in the year. I was struggling internally with my role as I struggled outwardly with my self-imposed standard to keep up physically with the pace set by the two college students on our team.

One of the first things we noticed about the village was that there was nothing to carry or transport heavy loads, other than an occasional bicycle that was piled high and pushed up and down the hilly road. There wasn't even a single wheelbarrow. How strange to be in a place that seemed to be frozen in some ancient time, totally dependent on physical stamina and strength. I was still too amazed by the demands of everyday living to delve into the hardships and fate of people who cannot keep up in this harsh environment due to illness, disabilities or advanced age.

Subsistence

8

We arrived in October, and by the time I left the village 15 days later, entire fields of corn and wheat were harvested, using only a few dull and well-worn hand tools. One day, the pastor of the Mwatasi church came by at breakfast to say she would be gone for the morning but she would see us later in the day. She was going to harvest wheat for a few hours. After she left, I asked the team if they would work without me and allow me to accompany the pastor out into the fields. I caught up with her near her home, and she did not willingly allow me to come along, but I was persistent.

Since I was going along, they had to find a knife for me to use, and no one has a drawer full of knives in their kitchen or a garage full of tools. Outfitted with a fourth knife borrowed from a neighbor woman, our motley little group set off in a line–the older woman who owned the field, the pastor's niece with her baby swaddled to her back with a cloth, the pastor, and me. The other women were easily balancing large baskets on their heads.

We walked past what looked like a little subdivision of clay houses that I had not seen before, tucked over the hill by the church. There were frequent exchanges of conversation with women in the homes as we passed by. I know only a few words in Swahili and their tribal language, HeHe, but I frequently caught the word "mzungu," so I knew they were talking about me, the white woman. As the path wound around the hills, further and further from the village, I was being led where no mzungu had walked before.

I came to understand that this odyssey was as enlightening for the Tanzanians as it was for me. Pastor Upendo, the only English-speaking of the women, frequently asked me if I was tired and offered to stop so we could rest. When we had been walking for over an hour, she turned to me and matter-of-factly said, "We can go back now if you are tired." Their pace was slow, and while the hills were steep, I wasn't at all winded, so I pressed her about why she was so concerned with me being tired. Finally she said, "But you do not walk in America. You drive cars." Not a question, it was a statement. Aha! Now the truth comes out about her reluctance to allow me to come along. We aren't the only ones with stereotypes. They were probably worried that they'd have to carry me back to the village, in addition to the harvested wheat!

That statement evolved into a wonderful conversation (translated by the pastor between English, HeHe and Swahili) about life in America, health and exercise. The women found it quite humorous that we actually walk for exercise and have exercise facilities where people go to work out.

We arrived at the field in an hour and a half. It was a steep, cone-shaped valley with the largest portion—probably 15 acres—planted in wheat, surrounded by smaller plots. A number of people were already scattered about within the field, and I learned that the woman who owns the field donates the land and crops to people who need it, particularly pastors, evangelists and others associated with various churches.

The young mother set her baby in a small cleared area among the wheat stalks, and spread the kanga that she had used to swaddle the child to her back over the top of the wheat for shade.

I was given a hand-woven basket and knife, and the pastor showed me that I should cut off the heads of the wheat with my knife and put them in my basket. The valley was so steep that we stood as though climbing a ladder, one foot on a higher rung than the other. We were not harvesting the stalks as it was too far to carry them back to the village. Normally stalks, too, would be cut, bundled and carried home to weave into mats.

This was a living lesson in subsistence agriculture, a term I knew but never understood at its core until that moment. Subsist: to remain or continue in existence. What we do today enables these people to live tomorrow, to continue to exist. It doesn't provide any excess or add to riches; it enables only continued existence. And there I stood among people far less educated than I, whose very life depended on getting this field of wheat harvested before an errant fire gobbled it up, and I couldn't even figure out which side of the blade on the old knife was the sharp side.

These humble and generous people, in their mismatched attire and worn-out shoes, speaking in several different tribal dialects…I, in the hiking boots and clothing made of high-tech wicking fabric, fluent in only one language… I was the baggage that they worried about holding them back today. Well, they would not be sorry; I became determined to be an extra laborer filling one more basket than they would have otherwise had. I enjoyed the solitude of my work, allowing time to begin processing this amazing experience.

At one point, Upendo came over to me and apologized for leaving me alone. She also told me that she and the woman near her were speaking in her home village's dialect, instead of HeHe or Swahili, because they didn't want the others to understand what they were saying. As if I could tell the difference! Then she admitted, "They do not know who is you and who is Lori (one of my teammates). They say you all look alike." Stifling my immediate response, I calmly told her that it would be easy if they looked at our hair—Lori has long hair and mine is short. She was happy with this simple means of differentiation and went back to pass on the information. I wondered what else they were saying about these wazungu who had invaded their village.

A Better Life

9

After two hours of work, Upendo told me it was time for the two of us to return to Mwatasi. The others would stay for the remainder of the day. When we reached this field, I had looked at its size and slope and thought, "No way!" While we were there I marveled at the effort it took to manually till and plant a field of this size, and became grateful that I could contribute to the work of the harvest. I would have loved to stay, as I was certain that Upendo would have if it weren't for the water project circus in the village. While my basket was not as full as hers, I had harvested a significant area. My basket was emptied into hers and then the two were nested together and lifted onto Upendo's head for the journey home. She also had a pink plastic basket with something inside it, which she had carried to the field inside the previously empty baskets. Since she was carrying the wheat, I asked her to allow me to carry the pink plastic basket, which I learned contained two precious cloth-wrapped bottles of Orange Fanta for our journey.

We walked only a short distance before meeting the older woman who had led us, the woman who owned the land and shared with so many. She had been digging potatoes in an adjoining field—a gift for our team in return for my work. I humbly recognized the disparity of that gift.

A small battle of wills erupted when I insisted on carrying the potatoes. After all, Upendo already had the basket of wheat on her head, but she of course took back the pink plastic refreshment basket when I took the potatoes. That was good, since I needed both hands to balance the potatoes on my head, then shift them from one shoulder to the other as we walked. Although no more than eight pounds, the potatoes were surprisingly heavy for my mzungu neck to support. Just before we were within sight of the village, at the final stream crossing, I could tell that Upendo was growing increasingly stressed about me carrying the potatoes. Recognizing that it would be a disgrace for her to allow her guest to do that work, I gave the potatoes to her to carry into the village along with the wheat.

Before that, about half-way back, we stopped under a grove of straight, tall eucalyptus trees to rest and sip our warm, but refreshing, Orange Fanta. I knew that this was a rare indulgence for Upendo and a precious expenditure for my benefit. We sat under the fragrant canopy and I thought about my husband and family and the gift of this day. It was painful for me to admit that I knew they were consumed with worry, wondering where I was, what I was doing, and whether I was safe. Yet their unconditional love allowed my soul the freedom it needs.

I was 9,000 miles away in a village with no modern means of communicating with home. How could I ever accurately convey how thankful I was to be in this place? The things that were emerging in me would have to wait to be shared, in time.

We sat in the shade, simply friends sharing our lives and pondering the issues. Under those trees, I learned about the not-so-visible problems in the village: alcoholism among the men fueled by the home brew; the exodus of the young people protesting the hard work of subsistence agriculture, fleeing to the cities for the promise of a better life; the lack of jobs in the cities; and the return of young women, especially, in caskets. Upendo shared that in the month before we arrived, one young woman was buried after a crude abortion and another died from AIDS. Both girls had fled to the city in search of a better life.

ENEZA

A better life—what is it, really? A better job? More money? More time?

Sitting on the hillside outside of a remote African village, it isn't hard to develop a list of very basic unmet needs, the fulfillment of which sustain life at its very core. Things like safe water, food, heat and dry shelter. Moving beyond just living, there is a laundry list of simple things that would make a much easier and better life: a wheelbarrow, well-bred seeds, fertilizer, tools, water at each house, electricity... I can see why young people want to escape from life in the village in search of something better.

I have truly believed for as long as I can remember that contentment is not the attainment of what we want, but the recognition of how much we already have. By any standards, I have a great life. It was not more "things" that I sought for that "better life". It wasn't my life that didn't quite measure up--it was me. If I could just work harder, longer, smarter, be more responsible, do more... somehow I would be better. How ironic that I had come to Africa, where life itself is a daily struggle, to eventually accept myself and allow my contribution and contentment to unfold.

Pink Sweater

10

During that first trip I was observing and meeting the people and having the conversations that would become the magnets for my return.

Benjamin, the elderly man who lives north of Magedelina and Jeremiah's house, is a respected elder both in the church and the village as a whole. He is neatly dressed, often laboring in heavy jobs at our work site in a suit coat or blazer and a knit stocking cap. He reminds me of my grandfather with his ready smile and twinkling eyes, his quiet and kind strength in a small body.

The Little Girl in the Pink Sweater, one among the pack of children who were around us every day. We knew them by their clothes, because they wore the same thing every day. She stood out, because she wore a beautiful little pink sweater with a white lace collar. I wondered how it had found its way to this primitive village in Africa. When I returned 7 months later, there she was again, her pink sweater no longer new, a bit more stretched out, the pink muted by 200 days of wear, and the lace hanging in several spots. I wondered if she and her friends thought when they saw me, "There's the mzungu woman again in the black pants and burgundy shirt."

The Woman at the Water Tap came out from her house with a pail as we tested the water system for leaks. She put her hands under the faucet, drank and splashed the water on her face. As she drank again, she said the Swahili word for sweet. Then she dropped to her knees and clasped her hands in prayer. With uninhibited joy and thanksgiving, she jumped up and danced all alone while her pail filled with clear, sweet water for the first time in her life. I think of her with great humility while brushing my teeth at the faucet in the sink in my bathroom. What a privilege to have shared that moment by the simple water tap alongside the dusty street.

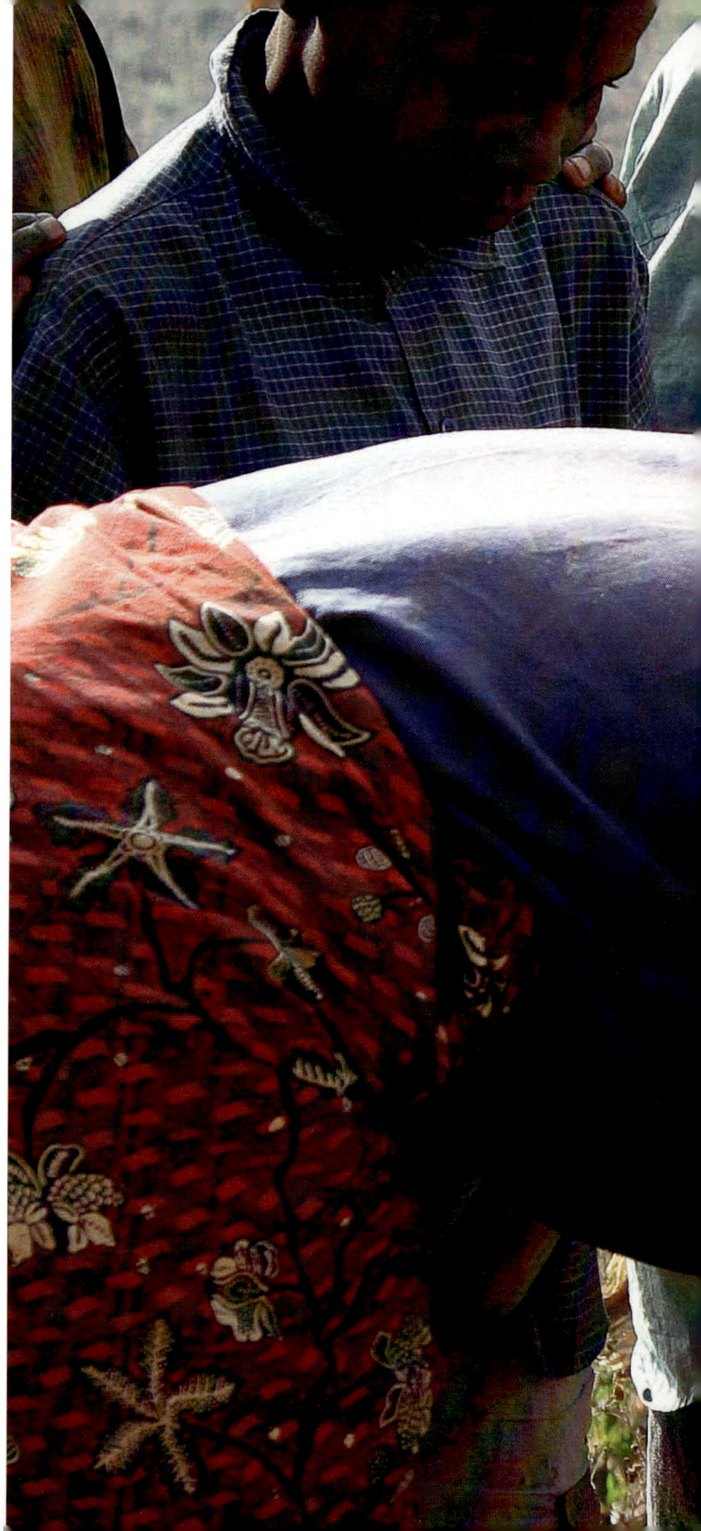

Alefesa –a dear friend, even though she can't speak a word of English nor I, Swahili. We met one of my first mornings in the village, when I took a different path up from the water hole that goes right through the courtyard behind her house. I surprised her as she was washing her morning dishes in a pan on the ground. It was a fateful and personal introduction to everyday life in the village.

Within the next few days, my teammate Lori and I were invited to join Pastor Upendo for an evening visit in a few homes, the first of which was Alefesa's. Just before dusk, we left our team working on the pump house, washed off the first few layers of dust from the workday and each wrapped a kanga around our waist for a skirt and another around our shoulders for a blouse/shawl. Upendo was visibly pleased when she came to meet us and declared that we looked like "proper Tanzanian women".

We entered the common room in Alefesa's house, similar to all the other houses I have since seen in the area. The basic wood chairs with their cloth-covered foam seat and back pads in this mud-brick house were adorned, as all of them are, with an embroidered or crocheted doily. Even though I've now made many trips to this area, I continue to be amazed by this touch of refinement in every home. These are homes and families that have none of the trappings that we consider absolute necessities for living: no water, no electricity, no cupboards, no dressers or closets. Yet on every chair is a touch of refined elegance that has been carefully washed and ironed over a cloth on the floor with what we would consider an antique iron, heated by placing coals from the cooking fire in the iron.

The room was dimly lit by a single kerosene lantern. We were served sweet tea in glass cups washed, I remembered, in a pan outside on the ground. The conversation began somewhat slowly, with Pastor Upendo's introduction of Alefesa as the congregation's Secretary of Women and Families. Then we just talked about our families, our jobs, our lives. The two youngest of her four boys were peeking at us from the doorway, along with a couple of neighbor children.

Later, as I became more trusted, I learned that the young woman with the sewing business along the street is Alefesa's daughter, Tusa, who also lives in the family home. Her full name is Tusajigwe, which means "we are blessed". Was that faith or a prayer? Tusa was born after the much younger, unmarried Alefesa met a man from another tribe, which appeared to be a pertinent fact as it was relayed.

Alefesa's husband is a butcher and she was interested that my husband was raising cattle. Their village has no electricity, no refrigerators, no Tupperware, no kitchen cupboards. When her husband butchers an animal, all the meat from it has to be sold and consumed immediately as they have no refrigeration—and no shortage of rats. Alefesa was amazed that we can keep meat for a year in our freezers.

How do you explain the concept of freezing to someone who has never seen a refrigerator, never seen an ice cube nor ever experienced a temperature capable of freezing meat? How do you explain water becoming a cold solid?

And then there's Oscar who lived in the house on the curve of the main street. At the time of our first trip, he was a 28-year old with some English skills and a natural talent for map-making. He had drawn maps of the area without the benefit of aerial photos, transits or GPS equipment, or even a bicycle. He taught confirmation classes at church and longed to complete Secondary School, the equivalent of our high school.

He and his shy wife had been married that year and proudly shared their wedding album with me when I was invited to their home for a visit. A year later, they introduced me to their baby son, Brian, and I took a family photo for them. Oscar had received a scholarship (through our congregation in Minnesota) to finish his Secondary School education and he was spending the weekdays at the Bomalang'ombe Secondary School, a 6 km cross-country walk away, walking home on the weekends to tend the fields and be with his wife and child.

He graduated in October 2007 while I was working at the Secondary School with one of our teams. What a privilege it was to shake the hand of this 30 year old man with so much initiative who gave so willingly to his community. He had no family at the ceremony as it was too far to walk with their child, and he was focused on studying for the government exams that were being administered the next week. Passing the exams is a requisite for any further schooling, and Oscar was hoping to become a teacher in Mwatasi's elementary school. I could tell he was barely allowing himself to celebrate the graduation.

Several months later when the results of the government exam arrived, Oscar's dream of continuing his education was stymied when he failed to pass one of the required subjects. He can study and retake that portion of the exam, but according to his school's custom, he would have to pay the exam fee on his own–another hurdle to overcome. For now, he continues to scratch out a living in subsistence farming.

But on that special graduation day, I gave Oscar a new spiral notebook and a letter in an envelope with the equivalent of $45 in Tshillings, breaking our established rule about not giving money to individuals. I received a letter some time later sharing incredulous thanks for the graduation gift that enabled him to roof the new house he built for his family. I knew that the gift could set a precedent with unhealthy expectations, but I took that risk because Oscar had given me so much more than that on my first trip to Mwatasi.

He and his wife invited me to their home for an evening visit with Pastor Upendo. They served us tea and we were each given a plate with rice on it, beautifully garnished with fresh shaved vegetables on top of the rice. It was an awkward predicament, as there were only two plates given to us without any for our hosts. They encouraged us to eat, and Pastor Upendo ate heartily while I carefully chose a few bites of the rice only. I explained that I had already eaten and was full, while the real reason was that I was certain to get sick from the uncooked vegetables prepared in the rudimentary kitchen. When I walked back to our team's quarters that night in the dark, I knew that I had received the most unselfish gift of all: our hosts didn't eat with us because they had graciously given their two guests all the food they had.

Benjamin, the Little Girl in the Pink Sweater, the Woman at the Water Tap, Alefesa, Oscar and so many more people I've been privileged to meet are with me every day. They are forever on the map; their faces in the photos are real; they are friends and family. While at first I could see only the differences, I now know we are more alike than different. They just happened to be born in a place that somehow got left behind the rest of the world.

They have shared their homes and their lives with me and I have witnessed and experienced joy and gratitude in indescribable proportions. I have seen them come running with buckets and anything that can hold water to gather all the water they can, because they thought surely this miracle cannot last. I have been in their schools with 70 children in a class, dressed in tattered uniforms, eagerly listening to the teacher. I have studied with a group of students preparing for their government exams. I have watched the progress over two and a half years as a man built his house, one handmade mud brick at a time.

They believe in the possibilities. They embrace the vision of a life that is more than merely surviving another day.

NIKE

BIBLIA

Choices

11

'Thy
will be
done on earth,
as it is in heaven.'

How many times have we recited that in the Lord's Prayer? Are we supposed to have a role in carrying out this will or are we just supposed to pray for someone else to do it?

The whole picture of need in the world is overwhelming, but I have learned that each of us can make a difference. And as these unexpected friends have made a difference in my life, I can make a difference in theirs. They need sustained encouragement and a few extra hands and tools to join theirs in developing the momentum and securing the education that will ensure a brighter future.

We have the ability and, because of that, the obligation to join hands with these very real people in this very real place and move together into a brighter tomorrow. What I never anticipated was the contentment and peace I have received in return.

Life is not lived in a straight line. Sometimes we start our day thinking we're going to St. Louis. Sometimes we end up in Africa. The roads in life aren't straight. But wherever we are on that journey, we have the ability to change—our direction, our perceptions and some of the world around us. Africa was the change of direction that enabled me to see the big view. I became fulfilled in a way I didn't even know I needed. I can be content with me. That contentment has given me the freedom to be present and embrace the possibilities. I no longer need the armor that hides my emotions and my humanness. After all, what's more interesting—a perfectly manicured expanse of lawn, or a rocky winding path? No matter how hard I try, I'm never going to be perfect. I have a better understanding of my strengths and have learned to give myself permission to use those to contribute what I can, with joy.

Each day brings multiple choices, many of which we don't even recognize. We can choose to keep learning and growing every day. All of our experiences build on each other to make us who we are. We can choose to be present for those whose path crosses ours, to listen, and when appropriate to share, for time and things seem to multiply when we give them away.

Sometimes the unexpected journeys provide the clearest view of all.

Epilogue

When we embarked on that first trip in October 2005 we were optimistic, determined and naïve. We did not realize how much we were undertaking, nor how ill-prepared the village was to maintain any kind of shared municipal service. Despite these shortcomings, the Mwatasi water system is still functioning and the village has grown in its understanding of local governance and responsibility. We were careful from the beginning to stress that the water system belongs to the village–not to the church, and certainly not to us. Guided by their elders, the villagers have ousted elected village officials who have been lazy or dishonest opportunists. Women stakeholders now have positions and representation on their Water Board. They have decided as a community how to pay for the diesel fuel that runs the generator for the water pumps.

Our congregation paid for and built, with their shared labor, the first two segments of the water system that provide water to nearly two-thirds of this village of 3000 people. The villagers themselves are building the next sections of the system that will serve the remaining third of the village. They have taken responsibility and initiative. We are the financiers for the system expansion, and they are utilizing the guidance of experienced local engineers from the nearby village of Bomalang'ombe. That village, "Boma", benefits from the dedicated economic development efforts of CEFA, an Italian-based European NGO, which has also become a good resource and partner for us.

The water project demonstrated our dedication and secured our credibility. The Tanzanians have come to understand that our goal is to partner on lasting solutions, not provide short-term aid. We have learned that both the problems and the solutions are complex and are seldom clear.

What has become clear, however, is that the key to sustainable improvements in life, self-sufficiency and poverty-reduction is education. In order to make a lasting difference, we must help people change their lives. We can't just fly in, build a water system, and leave, and believe that anything is going to change systemically.

Our focus has shifted from isolated development at a village level to facilitating sustainable Secondary School education infrastructure. Each school is comprised of students from numerous villages. What better way to plant, cultivate and harvest the seeds of a brighter future for multiple villages than through a strong education for eager and motivated young people at the Secondary School level?

The Tanzanian government's limited funds are allocated to providing Primary School education in most villages in their goal to make a Primary education available to all children. Concerns about classroom size in our U.S. schools are rather trivial in comparison to the sparsely-equipped classrooms I've observed in Tanzania with up to 80 attentive youngsters and one teacher.

When I see the maps, multiplication tables, electrical circuit diagrams, and anatomy lessons permanently painted on exterior walls of the Primary schools, I wonder if we would do so well with so little.

The government recognizes the importance of education to national development and promotes private investment in Secondary Schools to achieve their goals. To date, the private investment has been primarily through churches from the U.S. and Europe.

All schools are regulated and accredited by the government and classes are taught in English, which has vestiges of colonialism and also the global acceptance of English as a universal language. The schools have high standards; they simply have few resources with which to achieve those standards. In addition, nationwide, only 12% of young Tanzanians advance to a Secondary education.

Similar to that "Aha!" moment when the concept of subsistence agriculture became very real and personal to me, social justice came into focus for me at the Secondary Schools. Like the villages from which they draw their students, these boarding schools lack the most basic of infrastructure—water, adequate food, weatherproof buildings, electricity, and even books and paper.

We live in a truly global society where everyone should have access to the basics of life. With so much excess in some sectors, it is inexcusable that there are people who think that having access to safe, clean water is more than they can wish for in their lifetime, whose schools lack a single text book. Yet I have seen those same people kneel on a floor with an iron containing coals from their cooking fire to press a piece of clothing that had been hand laundered in a river. In those conditions, would we be concerned with ironing our clothes or having embroidered and pressed embellishments on our chairs? It is social justice that these people deserve the basics of life, including access to education.

I recently read the book "Cry, The Beloved Country" written in 1946 by South Africa native Alan Paton. There were so many parallels to what I witnessed 60 years later in Tanzania that one could easily retreat in despair. Yet, I am certain that for the first time in history, in this generation with our collaborative efforts, sustainable positive change can occur in African countries like Tanzania.

Why now? Since 1856 when the Portuguese controlled most of the East African coast, followed by the Germans in 1884 and the British in 1916, Tanzania has not been isolated from the outside world. What is different now that is going to change the very fabric and potential of the country and its people?

Global communication technology! Exposure to the possibilities!

When I first visited Mwatasi in 2005, it seemed trapped in an ancient time, despite the rare truck that drove through loaded with local lumber or corn, bound for Dar es Salaam. The quiet of the non-mechanized life was interrupted periodically by the putt-putt-putt of the one diesel-driven corn grinder, but the majority of women ground their flour by hand with a huge hand-hewn mortar and pestle. There wasn't a satellite dish or cell phone tower in the rural region. We had no communication with home while we were there.

One year later when we returned, cell phones were being charged in the Mwatasi pumphouse by the small solar panel that we had previously installed to power a small LED light. Cell towers were extending into the rural landscape and the cell phone market was flourishing. One team member found that he could stand in a specific place and call home with his U.S. phone.

In June 2007, I received a text message in Tanzania minutes after my mother came out of surgery at home. Upon our arrival in 2008, the huge satellite dish outside the house just below the Primary School in Mwatasi was too anomalous to miss in this village that is still without electricity. And by 2009, this remote area was captured in satellite imagery, no longer off the map to the rest of the world.

The young people, especially, who are hungry for knowledge and determined to have a better life, embrace the new technology and its capabilities. Poverty and geographical distance no longer control access to or outward dissemination of information. Text messaging, digital cameras and the internet allow us to span 9000 miles in seconds.

Mere technology, however, does not provide all the answers. The problems are complex. People can learn agriculture concepts that dramatically increase crop yield beyond the subsistence level, but without adequate roads that allow delivery of seeds and fertilizer in time for planting following the rain season and transportation of crops to market, economic development is stalled.

Government certification of Secondary Schools mandates teaching of all the familiar subjects, including math, physics, biology, chemistry, geography, history, and English. Tests are administered nationwide to strict standards. Students attend class daily and study diligently, often times by candle light or kerosene lantern. They pass the tests and advance to the next level if they are fortunate enough to have a scholarship or be able to work off the $350 annual tuition. Presently, only the top 12% have this opportunity because of the insufficient number of schools.

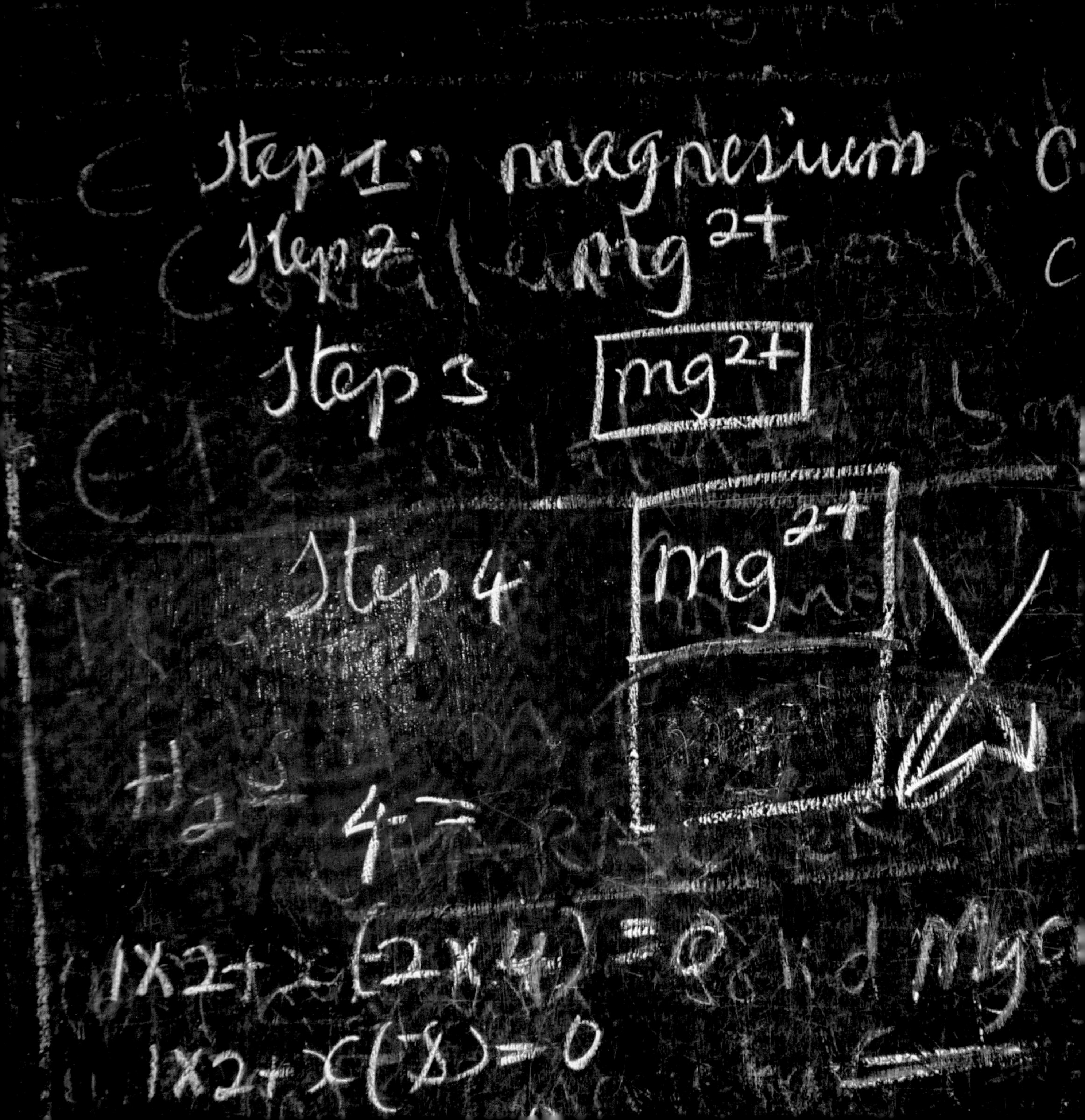
Step 1: magnesium
Step 2: mg2+
Step 3: mg2+
Step 4 mg2+
1x2+x(2x4)=0
1x2+x(-8)=0

Just imagine what it would take to accomplish that when your body is fed a thick glob of corn flour and water, topped once a day by watery boiled beans. And your mind has had to retain the answers to the questions through rote memorization, because your class lacks a single text book.

Yes, the problems are complex, but it all starts with education. The incremental improvements have begun and are aided by technology that makes us a global society. For the first time in history, we can help to make sustainable improvements in life that reach beyond face-to-face contacts, and spread across a nation and a continent that has been too long neglected.

Jim Collins illustrated the Flywheel Concept in his book, Good to Great. He explains that in its final state, any phenomenal change looks like a flywheel going at a very fast speed. The movement appears to be happening by itself, but starting the flywheel requires perseverance and steady force to turn the flywheel.

The Bomalang'ombe Secondary School is a flywheel. When I first visited in May 2006, there were 240 students living at this 4 year old remote school on top of a barren hillside. It had one classroom building and the students lived in temporary dorms made of slab wood that didn't keep out the rain during the rainy season, nor the incessant winds and the cold; temperatures drop to 45 degrees during June and July. The huge pots of ugali were prepared outdoors over an open fire fueled by wood gathered daily by the students over miles. They ate meals outdoors, sitting on the ground. Students started carrying water from the surface ponds below the school each day before dawn.

Despite those challenges, the young headmaster remained a visionary, strong leader and the students were motivated and engaged. The open school had been built with sheer willpower by the local diocese of the Tanzanian Lutheran Church–at the insistence and with the assistance of the local villagers, on land donated by the village. When the government official came for the school's certification inspection, the students were secretly sent away to sleep in the villages, as the shacks that looked like poor cattle sheds would never be approved dormitories for a boarding school.

In less than three years, with the partnership of a growing network of friends and an Italian economic development group (CEFA), the infrastructure of the school has been transformed. We worked side by side with students and villagers to trench a water pipeline that supplies safe, clean water from a CEFA site two kilometers away. Electricity generated by CEFA's hydroelectric dam powers lights at the school, over the poles that were laboriously erected by hand. The building projects have been expedited by access to water at centrally-located taps, as opposed to carrying it bucket by bucket from the bottom of the hills. (Making bricks and mixing cement and mortar a few hand-carried gallons of water at a time was an endless process.)

A private high school in New York provided much of the funding and assisted in building a huge new multipurpose kitchen and dining hall. The cooks can prepare meals with their new high-efficiency "rocket stoves" that are fueled by twigs and were designed and tested in a backyard in Minnesota. The girls' dormi-

tory, started with German financing, has been completed and the cardboard replaced by mylar windows transported in our luggage.

We paid for materials and assisted in building the boys' dormitory that is now complete. Parishioners from surrounding villages have begun building housing at the school for teachers, so the teachers will no longer have to walk miles to the school each day.

Finally, as I write this, I received emailed photos of the shipment of 1100 biology, chemistry and physics books that were delivered to the school through a grant from Rotary International. Microscopes, scales, test tubes, chemicals, a model of the human heart, and wall charts of the periodic table are being loaded into a shipping container with a generous discount from the supplier in New York.

The first corn crop is growing on the hillside under the guidance of the Minnesota-grown Institute of Agriculture and its new Tanzanian extension agents. Now that the school has the prerequisite water and electricity, once the crops are adequate, the experience of LiftKids (a nonprofit that creates small sustainable villages to feed, shelter and educate children) may help build a sustainable chicken egg operation that will improve students' diets with a consistent source of high-quality protein as well as providing supplemental income for the school. All of this has been achieved in less than three years by dedicated volunteers, with relatively small increments of personal funds and a single grant of $25,000.

The flywheel is gaining momentum. Sustainability is within reach for the Bomalang'ombe Secondary School, and plans are underway to assist with infrastructure development at six more schools in the district.

"Never doubt that a small group of thoughtful, committed citizens can change the world. Indeed, it is the only thing that ever has." This statement was made by Margaret Mead, an insightful social scientist and anthropologist born in 1901.

Now, more than ever, it is the time. We have the will, the resources and the technology to create a brighter future with the people of this neglected continent. We *can* change the future of the world, the world of our children's future.

Jacaranda trees are found in abundance in Eastern Africa. They have been called the tree of hope and faith because of the time that they bloom.

This area is subject to the harsh contrasts of a rainy season followed by a long drought. The Jacaranda tree blooms at the end of the dry season when the landscape is brown, near death, gasping for moisture.

When life is at its most difficult, the Jacaranda produces magnificent purple blossoms, steadfast in its faith that life-giving rains will come just at the right time. It infuses beauty in the parched landscape, trumpeting the change to come.

About the Author

Michele Hermansen is a dynamic, experienced leader who thrives on a full life. Her unplanned immersion in Africa development issues has greatly enriched her life and lives of people around her. Michele had previously been comfortable in a successful career that began in HR and progressed into sales and marketing. In addition to her work in Tanzania and motivational speaking, she is involved in local philanthropy as the part-time Executive Director for a Community Foundation. In her spare time she enjoys photography, horseback riding, and waterskiing. Parents to two grown daughters, Michele and her husband reside in New Richmond, Wisconsin. She returned from her seventh trip to Africa in November 2009.